NATIONAL GEOGRAPHIC

Working Hand in Hand

PIONEER EDITION

By Diane G. Silver

CONTENTS

Changing the Tide for Turtles

It's seven feet long. It can dive 3,000 feet.
It weighs almost 2,000 pounds.
What is it? A leatherback turtle!

José Urteaga (UHR-TAY-AH-GAH) stood on a beach in Nicaragua. He was a child. He watched baby sea turtles. They crawled across the sand. There were hundreds of them. They were going to the ocean.

Sea turtles are in danger. Fewer are being born. They could die out. They are endangered now.

José Urteaga is a National Geographic Emerging Explorer. He studies ocean animals. He knows that sea turtles are important to the environment. He wants to save them.

By Diane G. Silver

Turtle Hero. *Urteaga works to save sea turtles in Nicaragua.*

Urteaga knows that turtles are important to people, too. People in Nicaragua eat turtle eggs. It is a part of their way of life. Some people sell the eggs to **earn** money.

Urteaga knows the turtles need help. He thinks people should protect them. He also wants to help people in Nicaragua. He says, “I don’t just work with turtles. I work with people.”

Saving the Leatherbacks

Leatherbacks are Earth's biggest sea turtles. These gentle giants have lived on Earth for more than 100 million years. Now they are in danger. So are four other kinds of sea turtles. They nest, or lay eggs, in Nicaragua.

José Urteaga began to study sea turtles in 2002. He worked with the group Fauna & Flora International. He found very few nests of leatherback eggs. Most mother leatherbacks had stopped laying eggs.

Urteaga knew that these amazing animals were dying out. He wanted to know why. He found one answer. It's against the law to catch or hunt turtles. This is called **poaching**. But some people still did it.

People in Central America hunt sea turtles. They eat turtle meat. They also collect turtle eggs. The eggs are important food in Nicaragua.

Urteaga also knows people sell the eggs. The people sell them to **survive**.

Empty Nest. *People gather turtle eggs and sell them.*

Food Tradition. *People eat turtle meat for food. They have done this for a long time.*

Normally, these people live on less than $1.00 a day. They can earn $5.00 for twelve eggs.

How can Urteaga help both the turtles and the people?

Protect the Eggs

José Urteaga knows there will be no baby turtles without eggs. What should he do? Protect the eggs.

Urteaga has people guard the beach where leatherbacks lay eggs. The guards protect mother turtles when they come from the ocean.

Female turtles dig nests in the sand. Guards put plastic bags in the nests. The eggs land on the bags. Then guards take the eggs to a safe place. The baby turtles are born. Then people put them into the ocean.

More Problems for Turtles

Urteaga found other reasons turtles are in danger. People earn money from shark fishing. They use nets. These nets also catch sea turtles.

People build on beaches where turtles nest. Tourists damage nesting beaches, too.

Points of View

Guarding the nests saves the turtles. But that is not enough. Urteaga explains, "We can't only look at this from the turtle's point of view. We must also see the human side."

So Urteaga works with people. He finds new ways for them to make money. He teaches people to farm or raise bees. He shows them new ways to fish. He teaches them how to move trapped turtles from nets to the water.

Urteaga wants more people to know sea turtles. Then they will want to protect them. Families meet turtles at "Day of the Turtle" festivals. Urteaga hopes people will value turtles as much as he did as a child.

Sea Turtle Life Cycle

In the Sand

A sea turtle's life begins in the sand. Females dig nests there. Then they lay eggs.

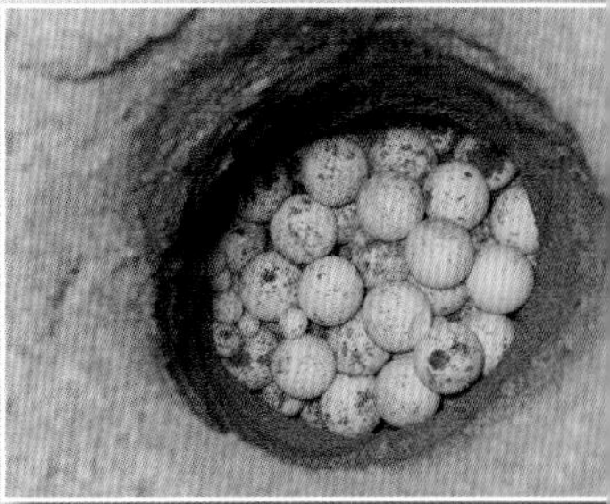

Digging Out

The baby turtles break out of their eggs. They dig to get out of the nests.

Into the Water

The baby turtles must get away from hungry birds and crabs. They hurry across the sand. They go to the ocean.

In the Open Sea

The baby turtles swim out into the ocean. They do not come back to land for many years. A sea turtle spends most of its life in the water.

Back to the Land

After 30 years, female turtles come back to land. They lay their eggs. Most mother turtles return to the same beach each year.

Beach Guards. *Urteaga and his team watch a leatherback turtle. It digs a nest. They keep it safe.*

From Poachers to Protectors

Urteaga changed turtles' lives. By 2010, his team protected three beaches. They put more than 34,000 baby turtles into the sea.

Urteaga changed the lives of Nicaraguans, too. Now more people know that sea turtles are in danger. Many work together to save sea turtles.

Some poachers now guard them. Many people want new ways to earn money. Some of them now save the turtle eggs.

Urteaga knows he does not save sea turtles alone. "I would never say that these **achievements** are ours alone," he explains. He says that many people work together to protect these animals.

Determined to Succeed

Sea turtles are still endangered. But the number of turtles is no longer dropping. People are proud to care for the turtles.

José Urteaga wants more people to help. So he must find more ways for them to earn money. He explains, "We haven't won the war. It may take the rest of my lifetime. But we are determined to succeed."

Wordwise

achievements: reaching a goal

earn: to receive money for work you do

poaching: catching or hunting animals when it is against the law

survive: to stay alive

Solutions for Success

José Urteaga is a creative problem solver. He gathers facts. Then he finds ways to solve the problems. Read the facts. Then read Urteaga's three strategies. Which plan is best? You decide.

The Facts

- Sea turtles in Nicaragua are dying out. We must protect the turtles and their eggs. But many people sell turtle meat and eggs to earn money.
- Nicaraguans eat turtle meat and eggs. They need the protein from them.
- People use nets to catch fish. Sea turtles get trapped in the nets and die.

Turtle hatchling

Circle hooks

Strategy A

Create new jobs!

Urteaga teaches people new ways to earn money. Some people guard the beaches. Some keep turtle eggs safe. Some learn to farm. Others raise bees. Some are guides.

Strategy B

Spread the word!

Urteaga wanted to tell people about the turtles. So rock stars gave concerts. They told people, "I don't eat turtle eggs." They reached over a million people.

Strategy C

Teach new ways to fish!

Urteaga's team teaches people how to save turtles from nets. The people learn about special circle-shaped fish hooks. The hooks are safer than nets.

TEAM Turtle

Five kinds of sea turtles live around Nicaragua. They are all in danger. Find out why each kind is special.

Leatherback Turtle

- **Claim to Fame:** It is the largest sea turtle on Earth.
- **Reason for Its Name:** Its shell feels like leather.
- **Size:** 4–7 feet (120–213 centimeters) long
- **Weight:** 440–2000 pounds (200–900 kilograms)
- **Food:** jellyfish
- **Fun Fact:** It can stay underwater for more than one hour.

Olive Ridley Turtle

- **Claim to Fame:** Thousands nest on the beach at the same time.
- **Reason for Its Name:** Its shell is olive green.
- **Size:** 2–2.5 feet (61–76 centimeters) long
- **Weight:** 77–100 pounds (35–45 kilograms)
- **Food:** shellfish
- **Fun Fact:** Its front flippers sometimes have an extra claw.

Green Sea Turtle

- **Claim to Fame:** It is the only sea turtle that doesn't eat meat.
- **Reason for Its Name:** Its skin has a greenish color.
- **Size:** 3–4 feet (91–120 centimeters) long
- **Weight:** 240–700 pounds (110–317 kilograms)
- **Food:** sea grass and algae
- **Fun Fact:** It cannot pull its head into its shell.

Loggerhead Turtle

- **Claim to Fame:** It has a strong jaw.
- **Reason for Its Name:** It has a large head.
- **Size:** 2.5–3 feet (76–91 centimeters) long
- **Weight:** 155–375 pounds (70–170 kilograms)
- **Food:** shellfish
- **Fun Fact:** Its shell has a heart shape.

Hawksbill Sea Turtle

- **Claim to Fame:** It has a colorful shell.
- **Reason for Its Name:** Its nose looks like the beak of a hawk.
- **Size:** 2–3.75 feet (61–114 centimeters) long
- **Weight:** 100–150 pounds (45–68 kilograms)
- **Food:** sponges, squid, shrimp
- **Fun Fact:** It uses its beak to grab food from tiny spaces.

Saving Elephants
One Village at a Time

The elephant is the largest land animal on Earth. Could it disappear forever? That almost happened in one part of Africa. Meet a man called "Hammer." He helped elephants. He helped his people, too.

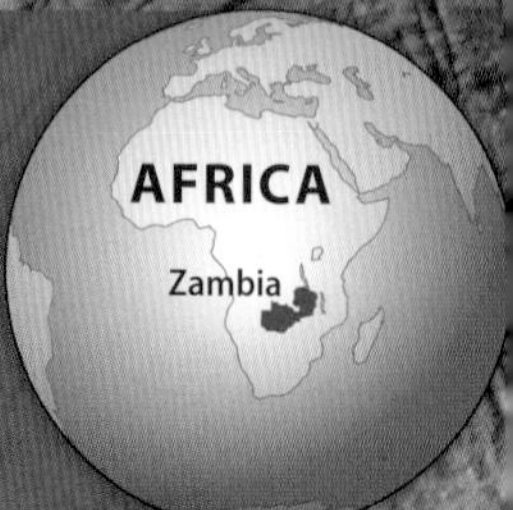

"No way! We can do this." When Hammer has a problem, he solves it.

A Man Called "Hammer"

Hammer's name is Hammerskjoeld (HOM-ur-shold) Simwinga. He was born in Zambia, Africa. He studied farming. He ran big farms, too. He also taught people how to garden.

Hammer was the right person to solve a problem in North Luangwa National Park. The park is in Zambia. Poachers were killing elephants in the park. They sold the meat and tusks. People pay a lot for ivory from tusks.

Years ago, 17,000 elephants lived in the park. Then people began poaching. Only about 1,300 elephants were left by 1994.

Problem Solver. *Hammer shows people new ways to earn money.*

Many poor villagers lived near the park. They worked for poachers. But soon the elephants would be gone. Their jobs would be gone, too. Hammer wanted to help both the elephants and the people.

One Village at a Time

In 1994, Hammer joined a project with Mark and Delia Owens. Hammer went from village to village. He taught new ways to earn money that didn't help poachers.

Hammer and his team gave some villagers sunflower seeds. They planted them. Then they made oil from the sunflowers. They used the oil to cook. They sold some oil, too.

People raised bees or fish. They had food to eat and sell. Hammer's ideas worked! People stopped working for poachers in 64 villages.

Hope for the Future

In villages today, "poaching is a thing of the past." Many people have new skills. Hammer says these people feel "their joy of life" again. And the number of elephants is growing, too.

Hammer believes people must protect Africa's environment. "If we wipe it out, we wipe out our future." The future can be better because of Hammer's work.

SOLUTIONS FOR THE FUTURE

Find out how people protect nature for the future. Then answer these questions.

1. How is José Urteaga helping both turtles and people in Nicaragua?

2. What does the author think of Urteaga's work? What do you think?

3. Which strategy on page 7 is best? Tell why you think so.

4. What problems did Hammer Simwinga help solve in North Luangwa National Park? How did he help?

5. How are José Urteaga and Hammer Simwinga alike? How are they different?